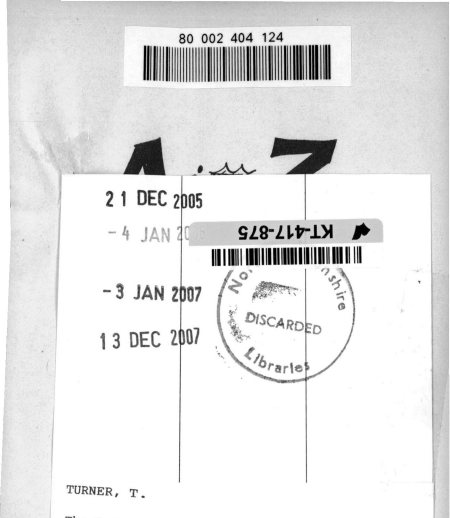

TURNER, T.

The A-Z of crackers, mistletoe and other
Christmas turkeys

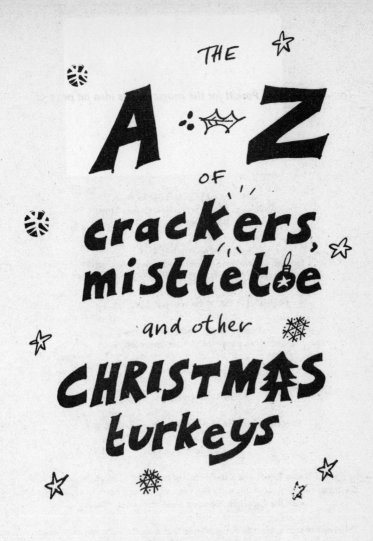

# THE A · Z

### OF

## crackers, mistletoe

### and other

## CHRISTMAS turkeys

**By Tracey Turner**

*Illustrated by Kate Sheppard*

**■SCHOLASTIC**

*Thanks to Kja... ...ge 54*

Scholastic Children's Books,
Commonwealth House, 1–19 New Oxford Street,
London WC1A 1NU, UK

A division of Scholastic Ltd
London ~ New York ~ Toronto ~ Sydney ~ Auckland
Mexico City ~ New Delhi ~ Hong Kong

Published in the UK by Scholastic Ltd, 2004

Text copyright © Tracey Turner, 2004
Illustrations copyright © Kate Sheppard, 2004

ISBN 0 439 96327 3

Printed and bound by AIT Nørhaven A/S, Denmark

2 4 6 8 10 9 7 5 3 1

# Contents

# Introduction

Do you love Christmas?

Or do you just put up with it to please your family?

Maybe you really don't like it at all and don't care
who knows it?

Whether or not Christmas is your favourite time of year, one thing's for sure: you can't avoid it. And, love it or hate it, what you need is a guide to making the most of it – complete with sackfuls of fascinating festive facts and silly seasonal things to do. So why not read on to discover:

- why Santa might put you in a bag and take you to Spain;
- the truth about sprouts;
- where you can meet a giant eel on Christmas Day;
- how to eat a candle;
- the world's most revolting Christmas recipe.

This book is full of information you'll be glad you found out – some of it useful and some of it very strange indeed. Simply start at "A" and carry on until you get to "Z" (or the other way round if you'd rather), and you'll be ready for a truly cracking Christmas.

# A

## Advent

Advent is where the fun begins, of course. It's the Christmas countdown, starting on the first Sunday after 30 November. Here are some Advent traditions you might want to try:

• Millions of us buy or make an Advent calendar and open a door every day in December up to Christmas. Make sure your calendar has some tasty treats behind each door.

• The first Sunday of Advent is known as Stir-up Sunday. This is the day you should be making your Christmas pudding (see *Plum pudding*). Making a Christmas pudding is a complicated business, so you might prefer to buy one from the supermarket instead.

• Maybe you've heard of a Bowl of Good Deeds? At the beginning of Advent, a bowl is filled with folded pieces of paper that have nice things to do written on them. Every morning until Christmas Day, each member of the family takes a piece of paper out of the bowl and carries out the good deed written on it. If this sounds a bit too nice for you, maybe you could have a Bowl of Practical Jokes (or even a Bowl of Corny Jokes) instead?

● Make 23 December trifle-making day. Try the incredibly messy recipe on pages 82 – 83.

### An Advent tradition to borrow

Tell your parents that you want to learn about other countries by sharing their Christmas traditions! In Holland and other parts of Europe, children get presents on the night of 5 December, the eve of the feast day of Saint Nicholas. And in France, Father Christmas pays a visit on the same night with small gifts and then turns up *again* on Christmas Eve with the big ones. See what response you get to the idea of two lots of presents – you never know, it might work.

Here's a tradition you might not be so keen on...

### Breakfast in bed with Saint Lucia

If you are Swedish and the eldest daughter in your family, on 13 December (the feast day of Saint Lucia) you're in for a special treat. You have to:

- Get up at dawn, before anyone else is awake.
- Dress up in a white gown with a red sash.
- Wear a leafy green wreath on your head with four lighted candles on it (one for each of the four Sundays in Advent).
- Make lots of delicious food and serve it as breakfast in bed to your parents while singing a special song.
- Lead a procession of carol-singing boys in top hats – assuming you haven't burned the house down by now with your hazardous headdress. Lucky you!

### An Advent superstition

*At the beginning of Advent, pick a small branch from a cherry tree and put it in some water. If the branch flowers before Christmas, it means good luck is coming your way.*

# Angels

See *Nativity plays*.

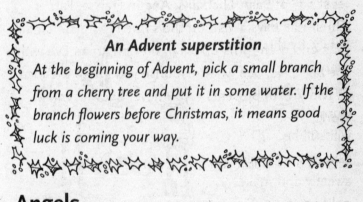

# Boxing Day

Things to do on Boxing Day (26 December) include:
- Watching telly and eating lots of food – a repeat performance of the day before but without the presents.
- Sneaking off to your room with your presents.
- Visiting relatives. This is very likely if you have a big family. By this time, everyone is probably feeling worn out, but you will still be expected to smile sweetly and make polite conversation.

- Pantomimes (see page 64).
- Lying around moaning because you ate too much the day before.

But Boxing Day doesn't get its name because people watch a lot of telly ("the box" – geddit?). It's because churches used to have "alms boxes", where money was collected throughout the year. On 26 December, the boxes were opened and the money given out to poor people.

If you were a servant in Victorian times, you'd expect to be given a thank-you present on Boxing Day. You'd probably be given the day off too. How kind! Your masters couldn't have done without you on Christmas Day, of course, so you'd have had to work then. (Up until quite recently, people who provided services, like postmen and postwomen, still received Boxing Day gifts.)

**A Boxing Day tradition we should bring back**
Perhaps you should be rewarded on Boxing Day for a service you've provided throughout the year – for example, all those times you did the washing-up without complaining (well, not much). Remind your

family that money is always a good choice for a Boxing Day gift.

**Feast day for furry friends**

Boxing Day is also known as Saint Stephen's Day. Saint Stephen is the patron saint of animals, and in some countries farmers leave out extra food for their animals on 26 December. So Fido and Tiddles should really get an extra dog biscuit or cat treat.

### *A smelly superstition*

*Boxing Day is the first of the 12 days of Christmas. During this period in Greece, ancient monsters called Kallikantzaroi are supposed to roam the earth making mischief. Superstitious Greeks burn old shoes to drive the Kallikantzaroi away ... and everyone else as well, probably.*

## Candles

See *Lights*.

## Cards

The first Christmas cards
were sold in England in
1843. Christmas is now
responsible for over
two billion bits of
post a year in
Britain alone (including 750,000 letters delivered to
Father Christmas).

Sending an adult a home-made card is a sure-fire
way to impress them. So at Christmas, why not
impress all the adults in your life at the same time?
Send the cards early enough and you might be in
time to get them feeling warmly towards you before
they buy your present. You'll be saving yourself
some money, too.

## An incredibly easy Christmas card

If you're not much good at drawing you can still make posh-looking Christmas cards really easily.

*You need*:
- Stiff paper or thin card
- A different type of paper or card – wrapping paper, corrugated paper, tissue paper, etc.
- Another different type of paper – preferably shiny wrapping paper
- Glue

*Instructions*:

**1** Decide how big you want to make your Christmas card and cut out a piece of thin card twice the size. Then fold it in half. (Doh!)

**2** Cut out a square from a different type of paper and glue it to the front of the card.

**3** Cut out a star shape from your shiny paper. Glue it to the middle of the square.

**4** Write your message inside the card.

**5** Er...

**6** ...That's it. Tricky, eh?

# Carols

There is no getting away from Christmas carols.
If you're not being forced to sing them in school
assembly or listen to them on the radio, then carol
singers are knocking on your door expecting you to
pay for the priviledge of hearing them strangle out
the wrong words to "Silent Night".

If you decide to go carol singing yourself, remember
that it is a good idea to:
● sing (in tune, if possible) rather than just saying
the words or humming; and
● know the words to at least one carol.
It's a sad fact that many carol singers don't follow
even these basic rules.

Of course, *some* people think it's very funny to sing the wrong words to carols. But *you* wouldn't be the sort of person to sing any of these alternative Christmas songs, would you?

### We Three Kings

*We three kings of Leicester Square*
*Selling ladies' underwear*
*They're fantastic, no elastic*
*Not very safe to wear.*

*Oooh-oh, star of wonder, star of light,*
*Someone set my pants alight,*
*I put them out, without a doubt*
*It gave us all a nasty fright.*

### Good King Wenceslas

*Good King Wenceslas looked out*
*On the feast of Stephen.*
*A snowball hit him on the snout*
*And made it all uneven.*
*Brightly shone his nose that night,*
*And the pain was cruel,*
*Till the doctor came in sight,*
*Riding on a mule.*

## Jingle Bells

*Jingle bells,*
*Batman smells,*
*Robin flew away.*
*The batmobile has lost its wheels*
*Now it's a bat-mo-sleigh.*

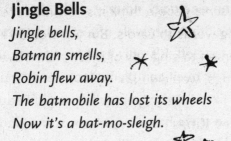

## While Shepherds Washed their Socks

*While shepherds washed their socks by night*
*All seated round the tub,*
*A bar of soap came tumbling down*
*And they began to scrub.*

# Charades

See *Games.*

# Christmas Day

The reason for all the presents, decorations and food is, of course, the Christian celebration of Jesus's birthday. But no one knows for sure exactly when Jesus was born, so why do people celebrate on 25 December? Well, imagine it's a very long time ago. There's no electricity, no telly, no lights and no central heating. It's the middle of December, you're freezing your toes off, it's only light for a few hours a day, and all the trees and plants look dead. You probably feel like cheering yourself up a bit. People always have, so there has always been some kind of winter festival in December. Christians decided to celebrate at the same time as the older festivals, and 25 December was first celebrated as the birthday of Christ around the middle of the fifth century.

## Christmas from ancient Rome

The ancient Romans had a huge festival called Saturnalia that started on 17 December and went on for a week or so. We have the Romans to thank for some of the ways we celebrate Christmas today. Saturnalia included:

- lots of eating and drinking;
- homes decorated with evergreen plants and candles;
- giving and receiving presents;
- schools and businesses closing for the holiday;
- general partying.

  Saturnalia also included a few traditions that haven't made it to the present day, such as the

sacrificing of young pigs at the temple of Saturn
(nowadays we sacrifice thousands of turkeys instead).

### A Roman tradition we should bring back

The Saturnalian celebrations included role-swapping.
For example, Roman
slaves were waited on
by their masters for a
day. Maybe you could
suggest this to your
school and swap
places with your
teacher on the
last day of term?

## Christmas is cancelled

Over the years, Christmas has been celebrated in
different ways, but in Britain it hasn't always been
the big holiday it is now. In fact, Christmas was
banned by the Puritan government in 1644.

Generally, the Puritans strongly disapproved of
any kind of fun, and they were determined that
Christmas should be a solemn occasion. You could
be arrested for hanging up holly decorations,
cooking Christmas food, or singing Christmas

carols! The ban lasted for 16 years, until Charles II became King of England, but the Puritans in America didn't celebrate Christmas again for more than 150 years!

### A brrrrrilliant Christmas Day tradition

For most of us, the main activities on Christmas Day are frenzied present-opening, over-eating, and watching lots of telly (and maybe, if you're unlucky, playing charades). But some people celebrate Christmas Day in a really unusual way: every Christmas morning in London's Hyde Park, brave swimmers compete for the Peter Pan Cup, which is given to the winner of a 100-metre race across the Serpentine lake. The temperature of the lake is usually around 4°C and sometimes the festive competitors have to break the ice before getting in!

### WARNING

*Whatever you do on Christmas Day, do NOT turn over a mattress. A Christmas superstition says that if you do this, you will die within the coming year!*

# Christmas dinner

Mmmm ... food – it's one of the things we most look forward to at Christmas. In Britain, Christmas dinner wouldn't be the same without turkey, Brussels sprouts, mince pies and Christmas pudding (see pages 84, 88, 56 and 28). But if you fancy a break with tradition, why not put one of these Christmas dinner dishes on your Christmas Day menu?

## Festive food from foreign lands

Want to try some...

- roast reindeer from Lapland?
- liver casserole from Finland?
- braised carp with gingerbread-and-beer sauce from Germany and Austria?
- curried goat from Jamaica?
- lutefisk – dried cod soaked in water and caustic soda until it begins to rot – from Finland? (This dish is not so popular now... I wonder why?)

- oysters and pâté de foie gras (goose-liver pâté) from France?
- pickled herring from Sweden?
- a seabird called Little Auk wrapped in sealskin from Greenland?
- roast giant eels fom Italy?

You might like the sound of some of those, but here's a revolting Christmas recipe from Iceland — eaten as a special holiday treat — that you definitely won't want to try.

## Recipe for hakarl

*Ingredients*:

One shark (dead)

*To make the hakarl*:

1 Gut shark, remove head, fins, teeth, etc.
2 Cut shark meat into big chunks.
3 Bury shark meat in gravel.
4 Wait for three months or so.
5 Remove shark meat from gravel. It should be nicely rotted by this time.
6 Hang meat in an airy drying shed until dry — around four months.
7 Cut off brown crust that has formed on meat.
8 Serve. Bon appétit!

# Christmas Eve

Christmas Eve is the night when Father Christmas comes down the chimney to deliver your presents – maybe you leave a mince pie and a glass of sherry out for him, as seven million of us do every year. (And if you live on a farm, you might leave out a bowl of gruel for the magic gnome who protects farms, as they do in Norway.) But visiting every home in the world in one night isn't easy – you should try it...

### Santa's accident-prone sleigh ride

Can you avoid the pitfalls of Santa's sleigh ride? Get some counters, a die and some friends and find out...

| 1 | 2 | 3 Reindeer off to a flying start – gallop forward 4 squares. |
|---|---|---|
| 12 Blown off course by a hurricane – go back 2 squares. | 11 | 10 |
| 13 | 14 | 15 Go back 4 squares for some dropped presents. |
| 24 | 23 Mince-pie overload – you get stuck in a chimney for the next 2 turns. | 22 |
| 25 WINNER! | | |

help

**BOO**

| 4 | 5 | 6 Surprised by small child and forced to hide in airing cupboard. Miss a go. |
|---|---|---|
| 9 Rudolph gets soot on his nose – you get lost and end up back on square 7. | 8 | 7 |
| 16 | 17 Caught speeding – miss a go while you pay the fine. | 18 |
| 21 | 20 | 19 Favourable tailwinds – move forward 3 squares. |

**A *Christmas Eve* superstition**

There are hundreds of superstitions about Christmas Eve. A Polish one says that if a girl grinds poppy seeds on Christmas Eve, she will soon marry. After dinner on the same evening, she should leave the house and listen hard. Her husband will come from the direction of the first dog's bark she hears.

# Christmas pudding

See *Plum pudding*.

# Christmas trees

If you've ever suffered from pine needles in your socks at Christmas time, Saint Boniface is probably the man to blame. Boniface was an English monk who went to Germany to spread Christianity in the seventh century. He explained the Holy Trinity (God the Father, God the Son, and God the Holy Spirit) using the triangular shape of a fir tree, and people began to regard fir trees as holy. By the twelfth century, Germans were using them to decorate their homes at Christmas ... but not quite the way we do now – the trees were hung upside-down from the ceiling.

Queen Victoria's husband, the German Prince Albert, brought the first Christmas tree to Britain (by this time, though, the trees had been turned the right way up and stood on the floor – which is probably just as well). In 1846, a popular newspaper pictured the royal family standing around their Christmas tree, and the idea caught on.

Today, most countries that celebrate Christmas have Christmas trees. But did you know:

• You don't find many fir trees in India, so people decorate mango and banana trees instead.

• Swedish Christmas trees usually have a goat next to them – to find out why, turn to page 76.

munch munch

• In Poland, Christmas trees are often left standing until 2 February – the feast day of Saint Mary of the Candle of Lightning. They must be knee-deep in pine needles by then!

## Crackers

Christmas dinner wouldn't be complete without Christmas crackers. They've been around for more than 150 years. But instead of the terrible jokes and riddles we groan at today, the first crackers contained soppy love poems. Hmmm, maybe those jokes aren't so bad after all...

Why not make your own crackers? It's easy and, since you get to decide what goes into them, pulling them will be a lot more fun. Remember, it doesn't matter too much what they look like – it's what's inside that counts.

## A cracking idea

*You need*:

- The cardboard inside of a loo roll
- Wrapping paper (or any kind of fairly thick paper)
- String, thread or ribbon (depending on how posh you want to be)
- Scissors
- Glue or sticky tape
- Cracker snappers (this is optional, but if you don't have them, you'll have to shout "Bang!" yourself when the crackers are pulled, which could be embarrassing)
- Things to put inside the crackers – see below for ideas

*To make the crackers*:

1 Cut out a piece of wrapping paper big enough to go around the loo roll and overlap each end by about 5 cm.

2 If you're using a cracker snapper, put that in the centre of the wrapping paper, then wrap the paper around the loo roll lengthways and glue or tape the join.

**3** Twist one end of the paper and tie with string, thread or ribbon.

**4** Put your goodies inside (see below), then twist the other end of the paper and tie that up too.

*Things to go in the crackers:*

● Paper hats – these are essential. Make them as simple as possible out of any kind of paper. Use your own head as a size guide, but remember to include some larger ones for adults (and big-heads).

● Wrapped sweets and nuts (ones with shells on).

● Plastic things you get in cereal packets or gifts from last year's crackers – the  weirder/more useless/rubbish-looking the better. When was the last time you found something to treasure in a cracker?

● Jokes – see pages 50 – 51 for some very bad ones that you could use.

● Fortunes – why not put fortunes, like the ones you get inside Chinese fortune cookies, into each cracker as well as a joke? Here are some silly ideas for your fortunes:

> You will receive an unwanted gift.

> Keep away from mistletoe.

> A large bird will play a part in your day.

> You will find something of value under a tree.

> Do not eat the sprouts.

> Remember: it's better to give than to receive.

> You will eat too much and feel ill.

> You need to change your socks more often.

• You might want to include Christmas quiz questions too – see pages 69 – 74.

## A big bang

If you want to go for the world record and make the biggest Christmas cracker ever, yours will have to be more than 55.5 metres long and 3.6 metres in diameter ... so maybe it's best not to bother.

# Decorations

Christmas decorations should be taken down by Twelfth Night (6 January), but there's no rule about when to put them up. Some people go Christmas crazy and put their decorations up before Halloween – and, of course, shops always put them up as early as possible (they have been spotted as early as September).

If you lived a few hundred years ago, your choice of Christmas decorations would have been limited to evergreen plants (see *Holly*). Now, of course, there are tinsel, glass and plastic baubles for the Christmas tree, fake snow, paperchains and Christmas lights (see page 53)... but it's still nice to have evergreens too (see page 46 for how to decorate your house for an ancient winter solstice!).

### *A knutty tradition you might want to borrow*

In Sweden, the date to take down Christmas decorations is not Twelfth Night but Saint Knut's day, which is 13 January. At Saint Knut's day parties, children dance around the Christmas tree (which is probably almost bald by this time) before eating all the goodies that are left on it (probably not very many) and then throwing the tree out. Why not suggest borrowing this tradition if you want to make Christmas last a bit longer?

# Egg-nog

A revolting, thick, yellow alcoholic drink made from raw egg yolk, sugar, cream, rum and brandy, which only ever gets drunk at Christmas by very unwise adults.

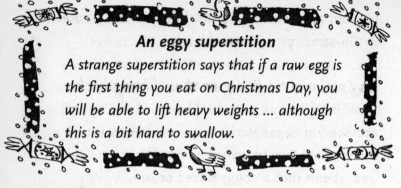

### An eggy superstition

*A strange superstition says that if a raw egg is the first thing you eat on Christmas Day, you will be able to lift heavy weights ... although this is a bit hard to swallow.*

# Epiphany

The Epiphany celebrates the Three Kings' arrival at the stable to visit the baby Jesus (see page 52). It's also known as Twelfth Night: the first day of Christmas is Boxing Day, so Twelfth Night is the night of 6 January.

If your family's superstitious, you'll take all of your Christmas decorations down by Twelfth Night. If you're not superstitious, you'll probably be sick of the sight of them and take them down anyway.

In some parts of the world, the Epiphany is a big holiday. In Mexico, it's the day when children get their presents (left by the Three Kings instead of Santa). In Russia, Baboushka (see page 40) arrives with her presents on 6 January, and so does the Italian version of Baboushka, La Befana. You could tell your family about it and try for a second round of Christmas gifts. It's worth a try...

### An Epiphany tradition we should bring back

Twelfth Night was party night in ye olde England, and the fun began with everyone eating special cakes called Twelfth cakes. Inside one of the cakes was a bean (not a soggy baked bean – a dried one). The person who got the cake with the bean inside it became King or Queen of the Bean, and they were put in charge of the party entertainment.

---

**A fishy superstition**

*Be glad you're not living in ye olde Ireland. On Twelfth Night, the tail of a herring used to be rubbed across the eyes of a child for good health throughout the year!*

---

# Father Christmas

Have you ever wondered what a jolly, red-suited old man with a white beard has to do with Christmas? To find out, we have to go back to the fourth century, when Saint Nicholas was a bishop who lived in Turkey (and no, that's not why we eat turkey on Christmas Day!). He was famous for being kind and generous, and one story goes that he left bags of gold in the stockings of a poor man and his three daughters. (So that's why we leave out stockings on Christmas Eve.) As the tradition of giving presents at Christmas grew, Christians decided that Saint Nicholas – or Santa Claus in some languages – was the obvious one to hand them out.

Over the years, Father Christmas has become famous for wearing a white beard and a red suit. In fact, the red suit comes from a Coke advert which appeared in the 1930s – before that, Santa dressed in green! Different ideas about the Christmas gift-giver can be found all over the world...

## Some alternative Santas

• In Holland, Sinterklaas is accompanied by a companion, Black Peter, who used to whip all the naughty children (he's stopped doing that in recent years, thankfully). Sinterklaas himself had a different punishment: if you'd been bad, he might put you in a bag and take you to Spain! You might be wondering why (and thinking that a nice Spanish holiday hardly seems like a punishment): it's because of the long history of wars between Holland and Spain – who knows what those nasty Spanish enemies might do to naughty Dutch children.

• The Finnish Joulupukki (which literally means "Christmas goat") used to be the opposite of Father Christmas – he demanded presents from people to stop him from doing horrible things to them. Nowadays, he's a reformed character and gives Christmas gifts – he's even given up his nasty habit of punishing bad children by hitting them with twigs.

• In Syria, gifts are given by the smallest of the Three Wise Men's camels. He must find wrapping the presents very tricky.

• In Iceland, there are 13 "Santas", known as "Jólasveinar". They are little elf-like people, with names such as Sausage Snatcher, Pot Licker, Candle Beggar, Door Slammer and Meat Hooker, who do slightly naughty things before leaving presents in children's shoes.

• In Russia, Baboushka delivers presents to children. The story goes that Baboushka was an old woman who was asked for directions by the Three Kings on their way to visit the baby Jesus. Naughty old Baboushka purposely gave them the wrong directions. Later, she felt ashamed of what she'd done, and to make up for it she gave out presents to all the children she could find. And she still does, on 6 January, the feast day of the Epiphany.

• Father Christmas's duties are done by a priest called a Hoteiosha in Japan. But watch out – he is believed to have eyes in the back of his head to catch out naughty children.

# Games

There are some parents who set cruel yule rules about entertainment on Christmas Day. Instead of letting you get on with your presents and the Christmas Day TV schedule, they insist on turning off the telly and forcing everyone to join in their idea of a hilariously good time: charades. A word that strikes fear into many hearts.

It might be that you are slightly odd and actually like charades. If so, congratulations. But if not, here are some alternative Christmas games that you might like to suggest playing instead...

## Balloon bursting

*Players*: At least two, but it must be an even number
*You need*: A blown-up balloon for each player; string; plenty of energy

*To play:*

**1** Players pair up into teams of two.

**2** Each player ties a balloon to his or her partner's left leg with string.

**3** Using the right leg, players try to burst their partner's balloon. Both players should try to burst their partner's balloon at the same time.

**4** Mayhem ensues for some time.

**5** The winner is the first person to burst the other player's balloon.

## Famous foreheads

*Players*: At least two

*You need*: Sticky tape; small slips of paper; pens

*To play:*

**1** Each player thinks of a famous person. This could be anyone, living or dead – Attila the Hun, Kylie Minogue, Prince Charles ... but make sure the people are famous enough for everyone playing to know who they are.

**2** Players write down their famous person on a slip of paper, then stick it on the forehead of the person to their right.

**3** All players will now have a famous person's name sticky-taped to their foreheads. Each player can see everyone else's famous person, but not his or her own (make sure there aren't any mirrors around).

**4** The player who ate the most at Christmas dinner goes first. He (or she) asks a "yes or no" question to try and find out the identity of his (or her) famous person. This could be, "Am I a man/woman?", "Am I dead/alive?", "Am I an entertainer?", "Am I a ruthless Mongol Emperor?", etc. Everyone else answers either "yes" or "no". If the answer to a question is "yes" the player can ask another question. When the answer to a question is "no" it's the turn of the next player.

**5** When a player thinks he knows his famous person, he can make a guess. Of course, if the answer is "no", then it's the next player's turn.

6 The first person to guess their famous person is the winner.

For other alternatives to charades, see the *Quiz* on pages 69 – 74 and *Santa's accident-prone sleigh ride* on pages 26 – 27.

## Do NOT try this at home

The Victorians' attitude towards safety was a bit different from ours. Their idea of a fun children's Christmas game was called Snap Dragons. The rules of play were simple: the adults put raisins into a bowl full of brandy. Then the children had to pick out the raisins – the one who got the most was the winner. This would have been a nice, easy game, were it not for the fact that the brandy was set on fire first! Yes – the poor kids had to risk burning their hands to win!

# Goose

Most people in Britain have *turkey* (see page 84) for Christmas dinner, but quite a lot of people eat a Christmas goose. The turkeys we eat are large, fat and flightless, while geese can fly and are famous for their vicious tempers ... maybe that's why more turkeys end up as lunch.

snap snap

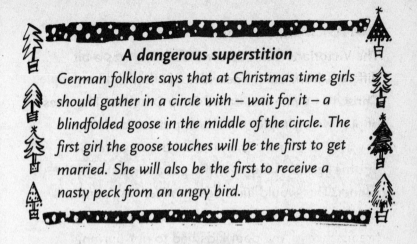

### *A dangerous superstition*

*German folklore says that at Christmas time girls should gather in a circle with – wait for it – a blindfolded goose in the middle of the circle. The first girl the goose touches will be the first to get married. She will also be the first to receive a nasty peck from an angry bird.*

# Grotto

It's a Christmas tradition for small children to pay a visit to Santa's grotto. Of course, if the small children had any sense they'd realize that it couldn't possibly be the real Santa – the high street is nowhere near the North Pole, after all, and why on earth would Father Christmas be holed up in Bogden's Department Store? And surely Santa has a real beard, not a mangy-looking false one? But not many young kids ask questions when presents are on the agenda (they don't yet know the woeful quality of Santa's gifts), and don't seem to mind that grottoes are almost always grotty.

### The real Santa's grotto

You might think of the North Pole as the place Father Christmas calls home. But the Finnish people are a lot more specific – according to them, he lives at a place called Korvatunturi in eastern Lapland.

# Holly

In the days before tinsel and giant inflatable snowmen, the only Christmas decorations were evergreen plants like holly and ivy. The ancient Romans, Celts, Vikings and Saxons all used them as decorations at their winter festivals.

### Winter solstice decorating tips

Why not go for a *really* old-fashioned Christmas and decorate your home for a traditional ancient winter solstice?

**1** Make sure you have a *yule log* (see page 92) burning in your fireplace.

**2** Bring a live tree into your home so that the wood spirits will have somewhere to keep warm during the coldest part of the year. Hang food among/on the branches, as well as little bells – if they ring, you'll know there's a spirit present.

**3** Put wreaths and garlands of evergreens such as holly, ivy and mistletoe around the place. They're symbols of new life and will bring you good luck. And the spiky leaves of the holly make another good hiding place for winter spirits.

**4** Oak stands for the new year, so scatter some acorns about as decoration.

**5** Wheat is important because it symbolizes the harvest. Make some straw figures to decorate your home, and throw some grain on the floor (you might have to make do with muesli).

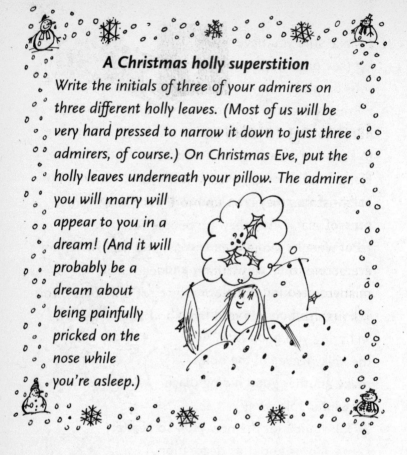

## A Christmas holly superstition

Write the initials of three of your admirers on three different holly leaves. (Most of us will be very hard pressed to narrow it down to just three admirers, of course.) On Christmas Eve, put the holly leaves underneath your pillow. The admirer you will marry will appear to you in a dream! (And it will probably be a dream about being painfully pricked on the nose while you're asleep.)

## A holly-ble fact

Boiled-up holly leaves are supposed to be a cure for worms (the kind that live in your insides)!

# Irritating relatives

There is seldom any escape from your relatives, but at Christmas they crop up more than at any other time of year. Often they are people you barely recognize, let alone want to kiss, and some of them are bound to be very irritating indeed. Irritating relatives are one of the downsides of Christmas. You will just have to grit your teeth and smile sweetly.

# Ivy

See *Holly*.

## Jokes

Sadly, the jokes you are most likely to hear at Christmas time come out of crackers. Sadly, because most of them are very bad jokes. Try putting some of these in your home-made Christmas crackers – they're bound to *sleigh* you (groan)...

Why is Santa like a bear on Christmas Eve?
*Because he's Sooty.*

*Oh, No!*

Which reindeer can jump higher than a house?
*They all can – houses can't jump.*

What beats its chest and swings from Christmas cake to Christmas cake?
*Tarzipan.*

How many chimneys does Father Christmas climb down?
*Stacks.*

*Cringe*

**stop!**

What happens if you eat the Christmas decorations?
*You get tinsel-itus.*

How do you make an idiot laugh on Boxing Day?
*Tell him a joke on Christmas Eve.*

What does Father Christmas get if he's stuck in a chimney?
*Santa Claustrophobia.*

**Wince**

How do snowmen travel around?
*By icicle.*

Who is never hungry at Christmas?
*The turkey – it's always stuffed.*

What goes "Ho! Ho! Ho! Thump!"?
*Father Christmas laughing his head off.*

What are a monkey's favourite songs?
*"Jungle Bells" and "King Kong Merrily on High".*

**That's enough! I can't take any more!**

# Kings

The Three Kings are a part of the Christmas story, and always feature in school *nativity plays* (see page 57). The day the Kings gave their presents to the baby Jesus is celebrated on 6 January (see *Epiphany*) – a bit late for the birthday, but then again they'd just travelled hundreds of miles by camel following a star, so we'll let them off. You might remember that the presents they gave were gold, frankincense (a kind of incense) and myrrh (a perfumed oil). Cuddly toys are a more usual choice for a newborn – incense sticks and essential oils are more the kind of thing you'd give your auntie. Sadly, the Bible doesn't record Mary and Joseph's reaction.

In fact, the Bible doesn't mention three kings at all: it says that wise men (or "Magi") were responsible for the odd gift selection. Over the years, the wise men became the Three Kings, called Caspar, Melchior and Balthasar. (If you find those names difficult to say, try the ones given them by a Syrian writer: Perozadh, Hormizdah and Yazdegerd!)

## Lights

In towns all over the world, the Christmas lights are turned on every year in a special ceremony – usually involving someone very slightly famous. For a few weeks, the local high street looks pretty and festive. It might even take your mind off the fact that it's freezing cold. Some people go a bit bonkers and try to recreate the public Christmas light extravaganza on the front of their house, often using thousands of light bulbs.

Before electricity, there were no outside Christmas lights and Christmas trees used to be lit with candles, which meant lots of nasty accidents. People tried to improve safety by putting their candles inside glass containers called fairy lamps, some of which were made to look like Queen Victoria. They were very pretty (except the ones that looked like Queen Victoria), but they still weren't all that safe. Today's fairy lights are named after the Victorian glass fairy lamps, and they are still causing nasty accidents. It's possible for fairy lights to set fire to the Christmas tree, so they should never be left on when there's no one around to keep an eye on them.

## Magic edible Christmas candles

If you've ever longed for a Christmas candle you can eat – and haven't we all? – look no further!

*You need*:

- A banana
- A walnut or peanut
- A friendly adult

*Instructions*:

1 Peel the banana.

2 Chop off the bottom so that it stands up. You

might want to shape the top to make the banana straight, like a candle. Put it on a plate.

**3** Stick a peanut or a piece of walnut into the top of the banana.

**4** Instruct your adult to light the nut with a match. They won't believe this is possible, and the nut might take a little while to catch fire, so you will have to be firm and your adult will have to be patient.

**5** Once the nut is lit, it will burn for quite some time and (if your banana shaping is any good) it'll look just like a candle!

**6** It is a good idea to call in some witnesses for this next bit: blow out the banana and then eat it. Your friends or relatives will be amazed! Explain that you have always enjoyed the taste of wax. Then tell them the truth before they take you to hospital.

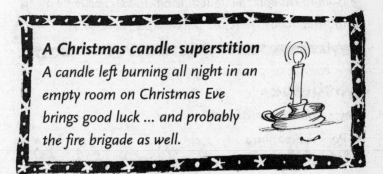

*A Christmas candle superstition*
*A candle left burning all night in an empty room on Christmas Eve brings good luck ... and probably the fire brigade as well.*

# Mince pies

In the Middle Ages, a mince pie might contain beef, suet (beef fat), lamb's tongue, mutton (sheep's meat), hare, rabbit, partridge, pheasant, nuts, spices and fruit. Thankfully, today we just stick to the nuts, spices and fruit, in a pastry case.

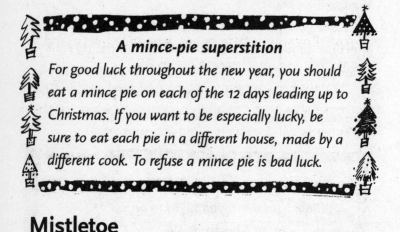

### A mince-pie superstition

*For good luck throughout the new year, you should eat a mince pie on each of the 12 days leading up to Christmas. If you want to be especially lucky, be sure to eat each pie in a different house, made by a different cook. To refuse a mince pie is bad luck.*

## Mistletoe
See *Under the mistletoe.*

# Nativity plays

You might well have been in a school nativity play. If not, and you feel like staging a nativity play of your own, these are the basic ingredients...

### The cast
*Mary*: Girl wearing a blue dress with a sheet over the top.

*Joseph*: Boy with a false beard, wearing sheets, and possibly a tea towel round his head.

*Shepherds*: Boys wearing sheets and tea towels. Try to make sure that not all the sheets are white, or the shepherds will look very similar to the angels.

*Angels*: Traditionally, girls wearing sheets and haloes (made from tinsel and coathangers). Girls usually end up as the angels in school nativity plays, but remember that the Angel Gabriel was a bloke. So why not break with tradition and have boys wearing sheets instead? Come to think of it, why not have a few female shepherds too?

*Innkeeper*: Boy or girl skilled at slamming the door to the inn without causing the scenery to collapse.

*The Three Kings*: Three boys wearing false beards, sheets and gold crowns made from cardboard and silver foil, and carrying empty boxes wrapped in Christmas paper.

*Baby Jesus*: Ancient plastic doll with no hair. Make sure there is plenty of swaddling (bandages or ripped-up sheets) to disguise this.

## The set

School or church-hall stage. No one expects flashy special effects, but you should at least manage to rig up some kind of scenery showing:

● the journey to Bethlehem (which can be used for the trips of Mary and Joseph, and the Three Kings);

● the inn;

● the stable. If you can engineer a moving star for the Three Kings to follow, your audience will be seriously impressed.

### The script

This can be very basic – in fact, the fewer lines there are the better. Use as many Christmas carols as possible to tell the story. "O Little Town of Bethlehem", "While Shepherds Watched Their Flocks by Night", "Away in a Manger" and "We Three Kings" are all good choices.

Remember, the audience is made up of your parents. They will think it's cute even if the scenery collapses and Joseph is sick over Mary due to stage fright.

# New Year

People have been celebrating New Year for thousands of years – it's probably the oldest ever excuse for a party. It was the Romans who decided on 1 January for New Year's Day. The month is named after the Roman god Janus, who has two faces – one looking back to the old year and one looking forward to the new ... which must be a bit awkward for him.

## New Year around the world

- The Scottish word for New Year – Hogmanay – comes from the ancient sun god Hogmagog. In Scotland and other parts of Britain, the first person to cross your threshold after midnight on New Year's Eve is very important: it must be a dark-haired man. If it's a man with red or blond hair, or a woman with hair of any colour, it's bad luck. Strangely, it's also important that the dark-haired man does not have flat feet and that he's carrying a lump of coal.

- In Greece, 1 January is Saint Basil's Day, when children get their Christmas presents (finally). Many Greek people celebrate New Year on 1 September instead.

- In Thailand, New Year is celebrated in April (lots of countries celebrate the New Year in the springtime). People throw buckets of water at one another as part of the celebrations.

• Watch out if you're in Wales, because the Cwn Annwn – ghostly black dogs of the underworld – are likely to roam about on New Year's Eve. Make sure you rattle and bang pots, pans and cutlery to keep them away.

• A beach in Brazil is the scene of an enormous New Year's party. Between two and three million people with lighted candles gather on Copacabana Beach in Rio de Janeiro. At midnight they leave flowers on the shore to be swept away by the waves as a gift to the African sea goddess Yemanja.

• The Chinese New Year is celebrated in February or March and the celebrations last 15 days. There are often huge, colourful processions and people make lots of noise with firecrackers to drive away evil spirits.

---

### New Year superstitions

*In Japan, people have a good laugh at the stroke of midnight on New Year's Eve to bring themselves good luck in the coming year. Dutch people might eat a doughnut at the same time for the same reason, while in Spain it's traditional to eat one grape on each of the 12 strokes of midnight.*

# (Number) ones

The Christmas number one is often the subject of debate, speculation and criticism. The songs that have topped the charts over the years have been a mixed bunch...

## Five festive number-one facts

**1** The Christmas number-one singer with the silliest name must be Conway Twitty. He topped the charts with "It's Only Make Believe" in 1958.

**2** Often voted the worst song of all time, "There's No One Quite Like Grandma", by Saint Winnifred's School Choir, was Christmas number one in 1980.

**3** Cliff Richard, known as the "Peter Pan of Pop", had a number one at Christmas in 1960, and two more in 1988 and 1990 – and, of course, he's still going strong today.

**4** The youngest person ever to have had a Christmas number one is Jimmy Osmond. He was nine years old when in 1972 he reached the top of the charts with "Long-haired Lover from Liverpool". (Find a wrinkly and see if they remember it – if they do, they'll tell you it was truly awful. They might even start singing it so remember your earplugs.)

**5** The Spice Girls had three Christmas number ones in three consecutive years – 1997, 1998 and 1999 – matching the record set by the Beatles over 30 years before.

## The ultimate number one

The biggest-selling Christmas song of all time is "White Christmas", sung by Bing Crosby. The single was first released more than 60 years ago, in 1942. It's sold over 100 million copies!

# Pantomimes

Pantomimes have been around for more than 200 years. They're a British Christmas tradition that people from other countries find very strange indeed ... and it's not difficult to see why:

● The pantomime dame – a middle-aged woman – is played by a man.

● The principal boy – usually the young man who is the star of the show – is played by a woman.

● Throwing custard pies is an essential part of the drama.

- There's always an obvious pantomime villain, and the audience is encouraged to boo and hiss at him.
- The audience joins in a lot – there's the booing and hissing, as well as a singalong, and people have been shouting "It's behind you!" and "Oh no, it isn't!" for the last 150 years.
- They use the same basic plots, based on fairytales – the two most popular are Cinderella and Aladdin.
- The pantomime horse (operated by two people inside a horse's costume) is another bizarre, yet essential, character.

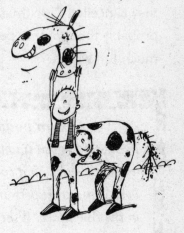

## Plum pudding

Plum pudding, or Christmas pudding, is the traditional ending to Christmas dinner – and part of the reason nobody feels very energetic late on Christmas Day. Christmas pud started off back in the Middle Ages as a kind of porridge, and over the years it's evolved into the rich, heavy pudding we know today.

Making one involves a ton of ingredients (including beef fat, or suet – yuck), and you have to leave it to mature for a few weeks before you cook it (which can take up to four hours!). But some people love Christmas pudding enough to go to all the effort.

Plum pudding was banned by the Puritans when they cancelled Christmas (see page 21). They probably thought that people were having far too much fun with it.

### A plum pudding superstition

In an old English tradition, a plum pudding would be stuck on a cow's horn on Christmas Eve. Some cruel person would then throw cider in the cow's face. If the pudding fell forward, it meant there would be a good harvest. And if the pudding ended up squashed all over the person who threw the cider, it meant the cow was very upset.

# Presents

If you are the Average British Person, you will spend 15 hours and walk 32 kilometres in your search for Christmas presents. And you'll spend between £300 and £400! Luckily, it's just adults who are expected to spend this sort of time, energy and money.

Hopefully Santa will bring you everything you would like this Christmas. But he's almost bound to bring you a few things that will horrify you. These might include novelty socks, a jumper with a hideous pattern, scratchy maroon-coloured slippers, or a truly dire CD that's impossible to exchange.

Be prepared for the Unwanted Gift — it is wise to practise your delighted gift-receiving smile in the mirror, and phrases such as "That's really unusual!" in a convincing voice during the weeks leading up to Christmas.

## Presents at a price

The Lithuanian Grandfather Christmas (Kaledu Senelis) gives presents to children on Christmas Eve, but the poor kids have to perform a song or poem before he'll hand them over. Imagine that – even worse than charades!

## *A Christmas present tradition we should borrow*

In Latvia, Father Christmas brings presents on each of the 12 days of Christmas, starting on Christmas Eve.

# Quiz

How much do you think you know about Christmas?
Take this festive test and find out. Then quiz your
relatives on Christmas Day and separate the
Christmas stars from the Christmas turkeys!

**1 Which of these is the name of one of Santa's
reindeer?**
**a)** Vixen
**b)** Viper
**c)** Vole

**2 The names of the Three Kings are...**
**a)** La-la, Dipsy and Po
**b)** Caspar, Melchior and Balthasar
**c)** Jasper, Malachite and Topaz

**3 On which day did Good King Wenceslas look out
in the Christmas carol?**
**a)** New Year's Eve

**b)** The Feast of Stephen
**c)** Boxing Day

**4 Who was the King of Judea in the Christmas nativity story?**
**a)** Heron
**b)** Hero
**c)** Herod

**5 What did "my true love" give to me on the seventh day of Christmas?**
**a)** Seven ducks a-quacking
**b)** Seven swans a-swimming
**c)** Seven turkeys a-gobbling

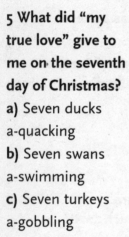

**6 When were the first Christmas cards sold?**
**a)** 1643
**b)** 1843
**c)** 1943

**7 In the words of the Christmas carol, "a lowly cattle shed" stood in which city?**
a) Royal David's city
b) Constantinople
c) Hull

**8 You should make sure you've taken down your Christmas decorations by which date?**
a) 26 December
b) 31 December
c) 6 January

**9 What's the name of Tiny Tim's family in Charles Dicken's story *A Christmas Carol*?**
a) Watchitt
b) Cratchitt
c) Scratchitt

**10 Santa Claus is named after which saint?**
a) Saint Claud
b) Saint Taclaus
c) Saint Nicholas

**11 What are baby turkeys called?**
a) Poults

**b)** Moults

**c)** Colts

**12 When is the Feast of the Epiphany?**

**a)** 6 January

**b)** The last Tuesday before Easter

**c)** 1 April

**13 What gifts did the Three Kings bring to the baby Jesus?**

**a)** Gold, silver and bronze

**b)** Gold, frankincense and myrrh

**c)** Slippers, socks and a jumper

**14 How many lords are "a-leaping" in the song?**

**a)** Five

**b)** Ten

**c)** Twelve

**15 Which royal first made Christmas trees popular in England?**

**a)** Queen Elizabeth II (the present Queen)

**b)** William the Conqueror (who became King in 1066)

**c)** Prince Albert (the husband of Queen Victoria)

**16 What is myrrh?**

**a)** An evergreen plant

**b)** A type of perfume

**c)** Bubble bath

**17 What does the Dutch Sinter Klaas ride on?**

**a)** A white horse

**b)** A white elephant

**c)** A sleigh pulled by reindeer

**18 In the nativity story, why do Mary and Joseph end up spending the night in a stable?**

**a)** They are animal lovers

**b)** It's warmer than a draughty room in an inn

**c)** There is no room at the inn

**19 The Christmas tree in Trafalgar Square in London is a gift every year from the people of which country?**

**a)** Norway

**b)** Sweden

**c)** Denmark

**20 What was a Victorian Goose Club?**

**a)** A hobby club for people who liked geese, which met every Christmas

**b)** A savings club, so that people had money to buy a goose to eat at Christmas

**c)** A club shaped like a goose that was used to bash Christmas turkeys over the head

*Answers*

1 a) (See opposite for the names of all of Santa's reindeer.) 2 b) 3 b) 4 c) 5 b) 6 b) 7 a) 8 c) 9 b) 10 c) 11 a) 12 a) 13 b) 14 b) 15 c) 16 b) 17 a) 18 c) 19 a) 20 b)

# Reindeer

Rudolph is the most famous of Santa's reindeer. The others are Dasher, Donner (or Donder), Dancer, Prancer, Cupid, Blitzen, Vixen, Comet, who were named in a nineteenth-century poem. Rudolph himself is over 100 years younger than the others – he was named in a story advertising a department store in 1939. Ten years later, the song "Rudolph the Red-nosed Reindeer" became the second-best-selling Christmas song ever, and made Rudolph and his shiny nose very famous indeed.

Reindeer don't always pull Santa's sleigh – in some countries it's pulled by goats.

The goat tradition comes from the Viking god Thor, who was said to be pulled through the sky by his two goats – legend has it that he lends them to Santa once a year. The Finnish Father Christmas sometimes delivers presents on a bicycle and sometimes on a goat called Ukko ... who is made of straw. The god Thor is also the reason you sometimes see straw goats under Swedish Christmas trees.

## Santa Claus

See *Father Christmas*.

## Scrooge

Charles Dickens' book *A Christmas Carol* has become the most well-known Christmas book ever.

Ebeneezer Scrooge, the miserly, miserable star of the book, is famous for hating the festive season, saying "Bah! Humbug!" to it, and thinking that anyone who says "Merry Christmas!" should be "boiled with his own pudding". Nice.

What about you? Do you say "Bah! Humbug!" to Christmas? Or are you a Christmas angel? Find out with this quiz...

## Scrooge – or Santa's little helper?

**1 You know your little brother wants a hamster for Christmas. You get him...**
**a)** A hamster, complete with cage, even though it blows your budget
**b)** A hamster, although it has to live in a shoe box for now
**c)** A pair of socks

**2 You hear a carol on the radio. Do you...**
**a)** Join in
**b)** Quite like it
**c)** Snarl and turn the radio off

**3 How many Christmas cards do you send
each year?**
**a)** Zero
**b)** One to ten
**c)** More than ten

**4 At Christmas time, you decorate your room with...**
**a)** Paperchains, tinsel and evergreens
**b)** Maybe the odd bit of tinsel
**c)** Scattered clothes, yoghurt pots with mould
growing in them, drinks cans, etc

**5 What's the next line of the well-known Christmas
carol that starts "We three kings of Orient are"?**
**a)** "Bearing gifts
we traverse afar"
**b)** "Wearing kilts
we travel by car"
**c)** "One in a taxi,
one in a car"

**6 What do you usually do under the mistletoe?**

**a)** Pucker up

**b)** Grit your teeth

**c)** A runner

**7 What's your favourite part of Christmas?**

**a)** Giving your presents

**b)** Opening your presents

**c)** When it's all over

**8 What do you do if someone suggests playing charades on Christmas Day?**

**a)** Shout "Hurray!" and start thinking of tricky movie titles

**b)** Sigh loudly, but go along with it

**c)** Turn up the TV and flatly refuse to join in

**9 What's your ideal role in the school nativity play?**

**a)** Mary or Joseph

**b)** An angel or a shepherd

**c)** Doing something else as far away from the school hall as possible

**10 You think Advent calendars...**
**a)** Are an essential part of Christmas
**b)** Contain some very tasty chocolates
**c)** Should be thrown in the bin

*Scoring*
If you scored more than five **a)s**: you are crazy about Christmas – but beware of becoming obsessed. If you scored mostly **b)s**: you are a well-adjusted individual unlikely to go bonkers at Christmas or any other time of year. If you scored more than five **c)s**: you really are a misery, aren't you?

# Sleigh
See page 25.

# Snowman

### How to build a snowman
If you're lucky enough to have a white Christmas, it is compulsory and masses of fun, to build a snowman. All you need is plenty of snow and some snowman accessories...

**1** The traditional snowman has three parts: a base, a centre and a head. Make three giant snowballs (as big as you can!), each one smaller than the last.

**2** Flatten the base of the biggest snowball and stand it firmly on the ground.

**3** Put the second snowball on top. Smooth over the join with more snow.

**4** Put the third snowball on top for the head and smooth over the join.

**5** Add a nose (a carrot is traditional), eyes (pieces of coal, stones, satsumas, etc), mouth (a twig, or a line of sweets or nuts) and twigs for arms.

**6** Dress with any available old clothing: a hat and scarf are traditional. Why not break with tradition and add a bikini top for a snowman with a difference?

# Stocking

See page 38.

# Trifle

Trifle is a much-loved part of the Christmas Day menu. Making one is a fantastic excuse to gorge yourself on cream and make a complete mess of the kitchen...

### Christmas trifle
*Ingredients*:
100 g trifle sponges
250 g raspberries, strawberries
or a mixture (fresh or frozen)
100 ml of your favourite fruit juice
500 g custard
300 ml double or whipping cream

Trifle topping: toasted flaked almonds, chopped nuts, grated chocolate or more fruit

*To make the trifle:*

1 Put the trifle sponges at the bottom of a glass bowl.

2 Pour over enough fruit juice – including any juice from the berries – to make the sponges nice and soggy. Drink any that's left over.

3 If using frozen fruit, make sure the fruit is thawed. Eat some of it, then put the rest on top of the sponges.

4 Eat some of the custard, then put the rest on top of the fruit.

5 In a big mixing bowl, whip the cream until it becomes light and fluffy, and thick enough not to fall off a spoon. This can take a little while and will mean you'll have to eat any of the cream that splashes out of the bowl – and maybe some that doesn't.

6 Spread the cream on top of the custard and decorate the trifle with nuts, chocolate or fruit – or a mixture of all of them. Make sure you taste everything to see which you like best.

# Turkey

Most people can't think of Christmas dinner without thinking of turkey – and every year in the UK we buy about ten million of the fat fowl. So you might be surprised to learn that eating turkey at Christmas time is quite a recent tradition. Christmas dinners of the past involved goose (which is still popular today – see page 44), pheasant, boar's head (a big hit with Henry VIII), swan and peacock (only for posh, rich people, of course)!

## Fowl facts

• Male turkeys are called "toms" (but female turkeys are just called "hens", rather boringly).
• Female turkeys don't "gobble" like the males – the noise they make is called a "click".
• Wild turkeys can run very fast – up to 40 km/h! Imagine chasing one of those for your Christmas dinner.
• Wild turkeys can fly (at speeds of up to 85 km/h), but most of the ones that we eat can't (which makes them a bit easier to catch).

flap flap ))

• Turkey has been eaten in space! Neil Armstrong and Buzz Aldrin, who were the first people on the moon, ate it as their first meal when they got there.

• Turkey meat contains a natural sedative called tryptophan – that's partly why you feel tired after your Christmas dinner.

## Twelfth Night

See *Epiphany*.

# Under the mistletoe

Druids (Celtic priests) are to blame for the tradition of bringing mistletoe indoors at Christmas time. So if you've ever had a nasty surprise under a sprig of the stuff, find a Druid and complain to him.

Mistletoe is an evergreen plant that lives on trees. The Druids believed that oak trees were holy, and that mistletoe growing on an oak tree contained the soul of the oak. In a special ceremony, they would cut down the mistletoe with a golden sickle. The cut mistletoe was supposed to protect everyone from harm in the coming year.

No one is really sure who to blame for the tradition of kissing under the mistletoe (so maybe you should go and apologize to your Druid). But here's a fact to put off any would-be kissers. Tell them, "Did you know that mistletoe gets its name because of bird poo?" People noticed

that the plant often tends to grow on tree branches
that have been used as a loo by mistle thrushes –
hence the name!" That should put them off.

### Mistletoe superstitions

A Swedish superstition says that a sprig of
mistletoe stops trolls from making mischief. And
in the north of England, farmers used to give
mistletoe to the cow who had the first calf of the
new year, to ensure the health of the herd.

oh no, not the mistletoe

# Vegetables

### Doubts about sprouts

Think of Christmas vegetables, and Brussels sprouts spring to mind. Lots of us moan about having to eat them on Christmas Day – so why do we torture ourselves? The reason sprouts are traditional at Christmas is simply  that they are one of the few vegetables that are ready to harvest at this time of year. Nowadays that doesn't matter, because we can grow all kinds of vegetables in heated greenhouses or import them from other countries ... so why we still insist on sprouts is a mystery.

Brussels sprouts have a slightly bitter taste, which is why lots of us don't like them. Here's another good reason for not eating them: they ferment in our insides and produce parps. (In fact, they're a good source of fibre and vitamins too – but don't tell your parents that.)

## The Night of the Radishes

The people of Oaxaca in Mexico must be very fond of radishes, because every 23 December they have a special event to celebrate the introduction of radishes to Mexico. People carve radishes into scenes from legends or the Bible, and a prize is given for the best carving. At the end of the Night of the Radishes, there's a huge firework display.

## A meatless treat

Vegetarians can have a hard time at Christmas. If you've ever tried hard, dried-out nut roast you'll know why. But some parts of the world have a meatless Christmas feast with a bit more style. In Lithuania, there are 12 delicious vegetarian dishes all served for Christmas dinner.

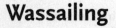

# Wassailing

The word "wassail" means "good health". In an old tradition, which still takes place in some parts of Britain, people carry a big bowl from door to door, singing for food and drink to be put inside it. Maybe you could try this out on your neighbours?

If you live near an apple orchard, you might like to try another wassailing tradition: pour cider on the roots of one of the apple trees on Twelfth Night while singing and banging pots and pans to drive away evil spirits. If that doesn't sound mad enough for you, a wassailing custom in South Wales, called the Mari Lwyd, involves a scary puppet made from a horse's skull!

# White Christmas

Whether you're likely to have a white Christmas depends a lot on where you live, of course. But why do we think of snow at Christmas time when Jesus was born in the Middle East – not famous for its snow at any time of year? It has a lot to do with all of the traditions that have become mixed up with the Christmas holiday. Lots of these traditions come from the winter festivals of northern Europe, where you are very likely to have a cold, snowy winter.

# Xmas

You might think that "Xmas" is just a shorter way of saying "Christmas"... and, of course, it is. But did you know that the X stands for the Greek letter "chi", which is the first letter of the Greek word for "Christ"? That's why we use it.

# Yule

"Yule" has become another way of saying Christmas, but the word originally comes from the name of an ancient winter festival.

### Cool yule log

An essential for your ancient winter solstice (see page 46) is a yule log, which can be either oak or pine. You should carve or draw a picture of the sun on it before lighting it in midwinter. As it burns, think of the coming warmer weather – if you don't, it might stay cold and dark for ever. Save a piece of the yule log to protect your home through the new year, and use it to light next year's yule log.

## The yule cat

Icelandic people who don't receive a new item of
clothing for Christmas are believed to have a
horrible fate in store – to be eaten by a monstrous
cat! The yule cat is a terrifying beast owned by Gryla,
the Icelandic mother of Sausage Snatcher and the
rest (see page 40).

The story of the yule cat began as a way of
encouraging people to work hard – wool workers
were rewarded with a new piece of clothing, but lazy
workers got nothing.

# Zips and zzzzzs

If you listen very carefully late on Christmas Day, you'll hear the rasping sound of zips being undone. It's the fault of Christmas dinner, of course – most of us will have eaten far too much of it and our stomachs expand for the extra grub.

As it gets later, listen even more carefully and you might hear snoring as people nod off in front of the telly. Because of all the extra work that our poor stomachs do to keep up with the extra food, and also because of the natural sedative in turkey (see page 85), everyone ends up dozing.

Maybe it's a good thing Christmas only comes once a year.

# Also in the A–Z series...

*Find out:*

- how to trick or treat, carve a pumpkin and other scary essentials

- what to do if you meet a werewolf

- some terrifying tales you might believe ... and a few you certainly won't